Let's Investigate with Nate

The Solar System

Written by Nate Ball   Illustrated by Wes Hargis

HARPER

An *Imprint of HarperCollins Publishers*

Dear Reader,

I'm often moving through the day in one of two modes—one is "Normal Mode," where I'm not in touch with the richness of the world. The other is "Wonder Mode"—and it's way more fun. In "Wonder Mode," the amazingness of the world pops out and shakes me by the shoulders, saying "Look at how incredible this is!" and I immediately want to investigate to learn more about it.

"Wonder Mode" is when I see the moon still visible in the morning sky and remember, "It's not just the moon that's in space—we're in space too!" It's when I look at the night sky with no telescope and see Mars and its red sparkle and think "We've sent robots there! What would it be like to go there in person?"

My hope is that this book provides you with new portals to view the world in "Wonder Mode" and to experience all the joy of discovery and learning that follows along with it.

Your friend,

Nate

HarperCollins
PUBLISHERS
Since 1817

Let's Investigate with Nate: The Solar System
Text copyright © 2017 by Nate Ball
Illustrations copyright © 2017 by Wes Hargis

Library of Congress Control Number: 2016949897
ISBN 978-0-06-235743-4 (trade bdg.)—ISBN 978-0-06-235742-7 (pbk.)

Typography by Whitney Manger
17 18 19 20 21 SCP 10 9 8 7 6 5 4 3 2 1

❖

First Edition

Every Saturday morning, the Science Museum opens to the public at ten a.m.

But every Saturday morning at nine a.m., before the front doors unlock and the ushers arrive for work . . . something magical happens! The Science Museum becomes a portal to adventure and discovery, and every Saturday, Wendy, Braden, Rosa, and Felix arrive at nine to investigate with Nate!

The Hall of Space has an old exhibit about the **solar system**.
It shows the Sun and nine **planets**.

Don't worry! We won't be earthbound for long. But first, let's talk about what makes a planet . . . a planet.

There are lots of objects in space. Some of them are planets, and some of them *aren't*—like **asteroids**, **moons**, and **stars**. But how do we know what's a planet and what isn't?

There's a *definition*.

The definition for "planet" was changed in 2006. Before 2006, the solar system had nine planets. Now, thanks to this new definition, it only has eight.

So the Science Museum's exhibit has to be updated.

Pluto is no longer a planet. That's what I hear, anyway.

Poor Pluto!

Are you sure it isn't a planet?

Yeah! How do they know?

Seems like we need to investigate—but the museum is going to open in an hour!

Good points. We'd better make sure. Let's investigate the solar system!

The Earth is big. Really big. It's about 4,000 miles from the center of the Earth to the surface of it! But the distance from the Earth to the Moon is a LOT longer than that. It's about 250,000 miles!

And the distance from the Earth to the Sun is even longer . . . it's almost 100,000,000 miles. That's 400 times longer than the distance from the Earth to the Moon!

But as far away as the Sun is . . . Pluto is way, way farther. If Nate and the Investigators were in a normal spacecraft, it would take them ten years to get there!

How high can you jump? Two feet? Maybe three?

Why? Because of **gravity**. And the more you weigh, the harder you have to work. So it's *really* hard to get a great big heavy spaceship full of Investigators off the ground . . . and into space!

BRADEN'S JOURNAL

Gravity is a force that pulls objects together. Every object in the universe pulls on every other object. The more **mass** an object has, the harder it pulls. For instance, because the Moon is so much smaller than Earth, it has less pull (or less gravity). That's why astronauts bounce when they walk on the Moon. Jupiter, on the other hand, is much more massive than Earth so it pulls harder. It has more gravity. If astronauts could land on Jupiter, they would be so heavy they wouldn't be able to stand up!

The pull from an object's gravity also gets stronger the closer you are to it. That's why the force from gravity is stronger when you're standing on Earth than when you're in a spaceship circling high above.

When we get to Pluto, the pull from Earth will be so weak, we won't even notice it!

Yes, but then the pull of Pluto's gravity will be much stronger . . .

Because we're closest to Pluto!

Pluto has much less mass than Earth. If we stand on it, we'll only weigh about one sixth of what we do at home.

A **satellite** is a machine that orbits the Earth. Satellites do lots of different jobs. Some of them take pictures. Others send television signals. Some of them look at the weather down on Earth . . . and others look at the stars out in space.

Hey, check it out! A satellite!

Wow! Can we stop and say hello?

Sure! Everyone, put on your space suits.

BEEP

BRADEN'S JOURNAL

An object in orbit travels in a path around another object. It keeps going around over and over again and follows the same path. For example, the Earth orbits the Sun. And the Moon orbits the Earth. Satellites orbit the Earth, too, and they do it the same way that the Moon does. Satellites don't have engines pushing them along. They use Earth's gravity to move! They're constantly falling, going around and around our planet.

SATURDAY 9:14 A.M.

When you stand on the Earth, gravity pulls you and the Earth together. The ground pushes up at you and you push down on the ground. When you're falling, the ground isn't there to push up at you. And so you don't feel your **weight**.

When you're in orbit around the Earth, you *feel* weightless, but you aren't really. The Earth's gravity is still pulling down on you as fast as you're traveling around. It's like you're falling in place.

Yikes! We're weightless!

I'm floating!

Actually, Felix, you're falling. Because we're in orbit right now. And orbiting is just a special way of falling!

Hi there, Satellite! So, what do you do?

Hi, kids! I measure how far away stars are.

Like those stars out there?

The Sun is a star, too, you know.

And those stars out there might have their own planets, just like our Sun does. Isn't that cool?

The group of planets, comets, asteroids, and other objects that orbit around our Sun make up the **solar system**. But that's not the only **planetary system**. Other stars have planetary systems, too. Lots of them! Every star is a huge ball of brightly shining, very hot gas. How huge? Our Sun has as much mass as 333,000 Earths! How hot? The surface of the Sun is about 10,000° F! It glows so brightly because of how very hot it is.

BRADEN'S JOURNAL
A group of objects orbiting around a star = planetary system.
A group of stars all orbiting around a central point = **galaxy.** Some galaxies are small—just 1,000 stars. Some are huge—hundreds of trillions of stars. **The Milky Way** (that's our galaxy) has hundreds of billions of stars, and our own solar system is just one of many planetary systems in the Milky Way.

The Moon is also a satellite of Earth, but it's a natural satellite. That means humans didn't put it there. Nobody is certain where the Moon came from. Many people think it was formed when something big smashed into the Earth a very long time ago. Bits of Earth broke off gradually and formed the Moon. But nobody knows for sure.

Because it's much smaller than the Earth, the Moon has less gravity. That means if you're walking on the Moon, you weigh less than you do when you're on the Earth!

BRADEN'S JOURNAL

How far apart are the Sun and planets? That's another thing that's hard to picture.
If I really wanted to show the whole solar system, some of the planets would be too small to see!

—SATURN   —URANUS   —NEPTUNE   ○ PLUTO

Stars and planets have lifetimes, just like you and me. When a planetary system forms around a star, that's when the planets themselves are formed. Usually a planet starts out as many smaller objects, or even as a cloud of dust. But gravity pulls them together into one big object—a planet.

Oh, to be young again. Why, I remember when I was just a little baby planet . . .

DEFINITION of PLANET:
2) An object has to CLEAR ITS NEIGHBORHOOD of other objects in order to be a planet.

My neighborhood is good and cleared except for my two moons. And to tell the truth, I'd be pretty lonely without them!

Planets can be babies?

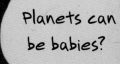

BRADEN'S JOURNAL
There are lots of asteroids in the solar system. An **asteroid belt** has a whole lot of asteroids in one spot.

An asteroid is an object in the solar system that isn't a planet, a **comet**, or a **meteoroid**. There are lots of different sizes and shapes of asteroids. But there is one thing they have in common: they (mostly) aren't round.

Jupiter is the largest planet in the solar system. If you put all the other planets together, they still wouldn't be as big as Jupiter. And it doesn't just have one moon, like the Earth does ... it has almost seventy of them! But there's something else about Jupiter that's different from the planets we've seen so far ...

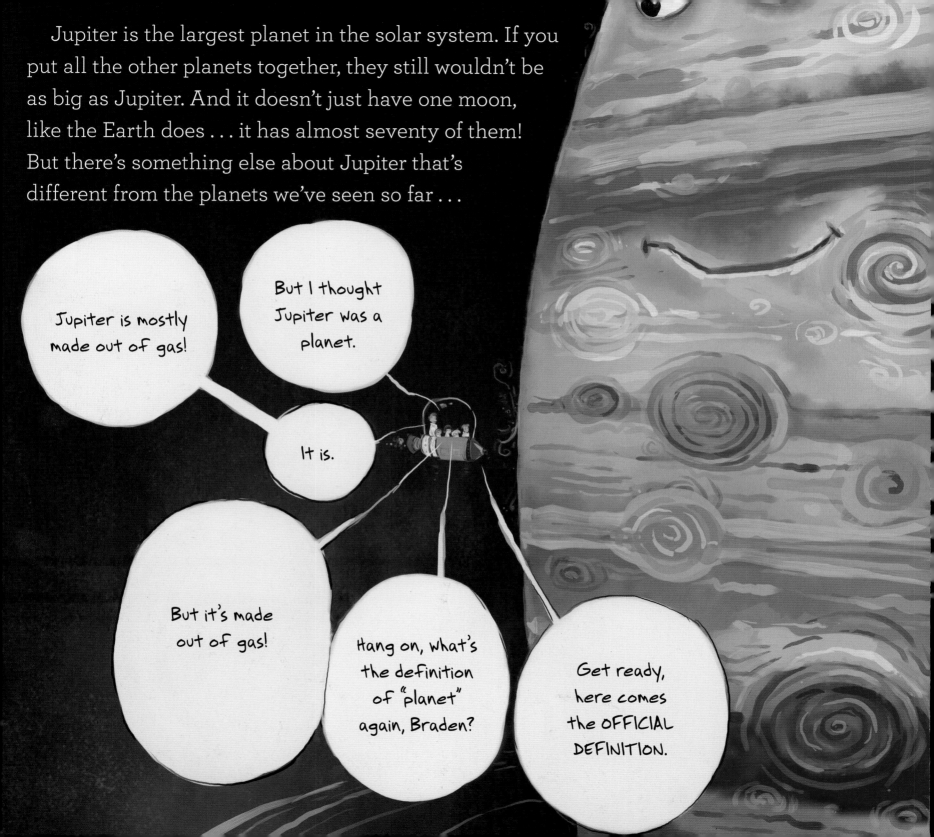

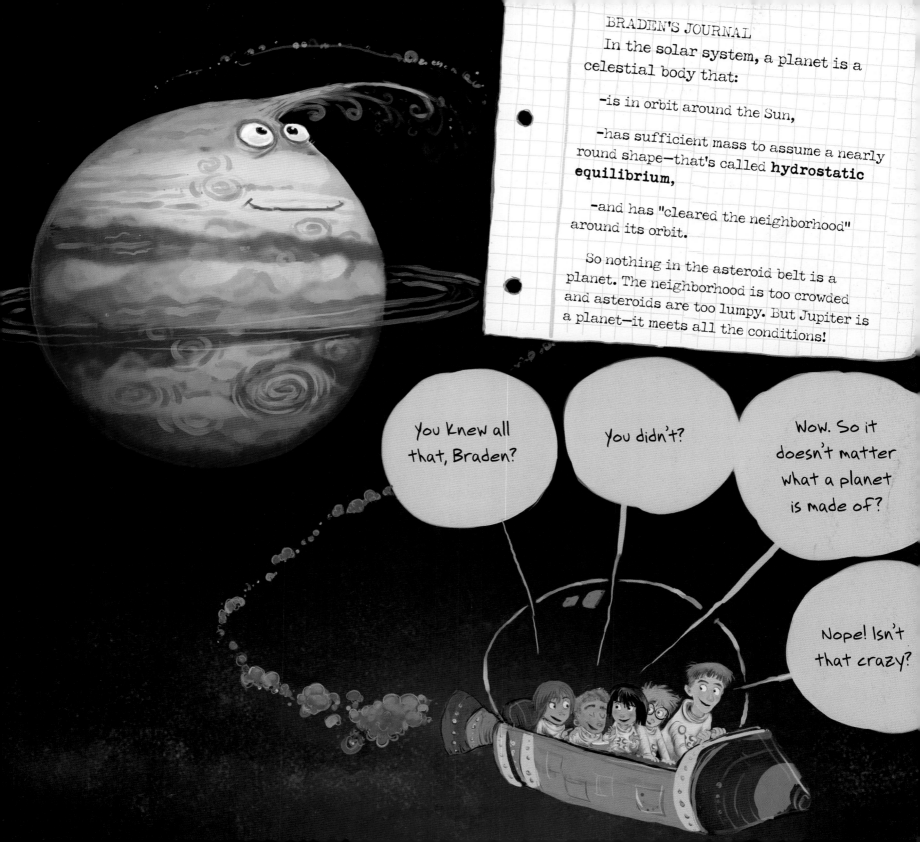

BRADEN'S JOURNAL
In the solar system, a planet is a celestial body that:

-is in orbit around the Sun,

-has sufficient mass to assume a nearly round shape—that's called **hydrostatic equilibrium,**

-and has "cleared the neighborhood" around its orbit.

So nothing in the asteroid belt is a planet. The neighborhood is too crowded and asteroids are too lumpy. But Jupiter is a planet—it meets all the conditions!

You knew all that, Braden?

You didn't?

Wow. So it doesn't matter what a planet is made of?

Nope! Isn't that crazy?

Between Jupiter and Pluto there are three planets. Saturn, Uranus, and Neptune are all made out of gas as well.

NEPTUNE

URANUS

BRADEN'S JOURNAL
Check out those rings around Saturn! They're made out of tiny particles of ice, dust, and rock.

What about their moons?

Moons don't count, even though some of their moons are really big.

So what does that tell us?

Saturn, Uranus, and Neptune are all planets!

BRADEN'S JOURNAL
Neptune's blue color makes it look like it has liquid water on it, just like Earth. That blue is actually from the methane gas at its surface!

BRADEN'S JOURNAL
Uranus looks boring, but it's not. The wind at the surface of this planet can blow over 500 miles per hour!

Pluto is the largest object in the **Kuiper belt**, which is like the asteroid belt but even bigger. That means that Pluto shares its orbit around the Sun with many other objects.

KUIPER BELT

CHARON

PLUTO

STYX

KERBEROS

NIX

HYDRA

Well, here we are! Pluto.

Brr.

It's really cold this far from the Sun.

It's time for the kids to decide for themselves whether Pluto is a planet or not.
But first, what do *you* think?

NATE

I feel so light on my feet!

What are those other things?

They look like asteroids. Some almost look like planets.

Definitions aren't facts. Facts never change, but definitions do.
Facts aren't invented by human beings, but definitions are.

Definitions help us to talk about things clearly. You and I both know
that the definition of "kitten" is "a cat less than a few months old." But if
we suddenly stopped using the word "kitten," it wouldn't change the fact
that your pet is a super-cute three-month-old cat.

In 2006, *something* changed, but it wasn't the facts, and it wasn't Pluto.
It was just the definition of what it means to share your orbit.

. . . when we investigate with Nate!

Another investigation is complete! And now the museum is perfect again, thanks to Nate and the Investigators.

**Important:
Ask an adult
for help!**

Experiment: Make Your Own Gravity Slingshot

Have you ever wondered how we get robots and satellites so far out into space? Rockets help, but they're only part of the story. To get a spacecraft going fast enough to reach a faraway target like Pluto in a reasonable amount of time ("only" ten years to go almost four billion miles), we use a technique called the "gravity assist," or even better, the "gravity slingshot."

Can we learn how a gravity slingshot works even without having to go to space? Yes, we can! And we'll do it by investigating.

You will need:

- an adult
- a marble
- a small cardboard box
- scissors
- tape (duct tape is usually best)
- a tapered plastic container, like a quart-size yogurt container (rinsed)
- a paper towel tube

Step 1: Have the adult help you safely cut the top rim of the yogurt container off. Make sure it's about half an inch long. It should look like a circle. Cut off one third of the circle to use as an orbital path. Next cut away the bottom half inch of the yogurt container, which we'll call the planet. The marble should easily fit between the piece we created as an orbital path and our planet. If possible, position the planet and the path so the entry point between them is wider than the exit. Tape them to a cardboard base cut from the box.

Step 2: Cut the paper towel tube lengthwise so it's like a trough. Fold the trough so it makes a V shape that will more carefully guide the marble. To turn the trough into a ramp that gently slopes downward, bend one end under. That creates the top of the ramp, and the other end will be placed at the entry point of the orbital path. Tape everything in place.

Step 3: Time for a test! Place the marble at the top of the ramp and let it roll down. Does it easily pass through the planet's "orbit" and exit out the other side? If so, we're ready for the final steps. If not, adjust the spacing or alignment of the different pieces, so the marble satellite can travel all the way through.

Step 4: Once the marble satellite can roll along the orbital path using only the speed it picks up by going down the gentle slope of the ramp, we're ready to test!

Testing

Now we can use our apparatus (a fancy word for "setup") to see how a gravity slingshot works.

The marble is our satellite. The gentle ramp gives the satellite a trajectory, or special direction, toward the planet. The inner cup is the planet, and the outer guide acts like gravity, helping the marble "orbit" the planet while gravity's pull is strong enough.

Place the marble at the top of the ramp and let it roll down through the "orbit" and out. Watch the speed of the marble's exit when the planet is moving. On your next try, sweep the ramp at a constant speed. What did you observe? Compare the marble's exit speed to when it went through without the planet's motion. What happened? What does this tell us about our hypothesis? Be patient and persistent, and most importantly, be methodical as you work.

With practice, you should be able to get the planet to add a lot of speed to the satellite!

Now think about all the amazing things humans have accomplished in space. We've learned how to shoot a satellite on exactly the right exit trajectory so it doesn't miss a target millions of miles away! Incredible! Can you think up an experiment to let you shoot a marble satellite from one slingshot to another? Get out there and try it, Investigators!

—Nate

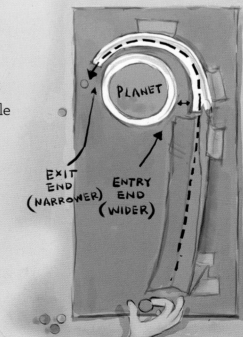

EXIT END (NARROWER)

PLANET

ENTRY END (WIDER)

GLOSSARY

ASTEROID
A small, rocky body less than 620 miles in diameter that orbits the Sun.

ASTEROID BELT
An area with lots of asteroids.

ATMOSPHERE
The gases surrounding any celestial body that are held in place by gravity.

COMET
A celestial body that orbits the Sun in an elongated path, made of water, gas, and dust.

GALAXY
A group of stars all orbiting around a central point.

GRAVITY
A force of attraction that pulls any two objects in the universe together. Every object in the universe exerts gravity on every other object.

HYDROSTATIC EQUILIBRIUM
When the inward pressure is balanced by the outward pressure. Generally, this results in a body having a spherical shape, such as a planet or a balloon.

KUIPER BELT
It's like an asteroid belt, but far larger, and it extends beyond the planets in our solar system.

MASS
A measure of the amount of matter in an object. Objects with mass exert gravity on each other.

METEOR
A meteoroid that has entered the Earth's atmosphere.

METEOROID
Any small body that is traveling through space.

THE MILKY WAY
The spiral galaxy, made up of more than 200 billion stars, that contains our solar system.

MOON
Any natural satellite orbiting a planet.

ORBIT
The curved path a natural or artificial satellite follows around another body due to the force of gravity.

PLANET
A large celestial body that revolves around a star, but does not produce its own light. The eight planets in our solar system are Mercury, Venus, Earth, Mars, Jupiter, Saturn, Uranus, and Neptune.

PLANETARY SYSTEM
A set of gravitationally bound celestial bodies that orbit around a star.

SATELLITE
A small body in orbit around a larger body.

SOLAR SYSTEM
It's a planetary system where the planets orbit the Sun.

STAR
Any celestial object that is visible in the clear night sky as a point of light.

VACUUM
A space where all matter, especially air, has been removed.

WEIGHT
The heaviness of an object; the force exerted on a mass by gravity.